budgetbooks

ACOUSTIC

ISBN 978-1-4234-7008-3

HAL•LEONARD®
CORPORATION
7777 W. BLUEMOUND RD. P.O. BOX 13819 MILWAUKEE, WI 53213

Visit Hal Leonard Online at
www.halleonard.com

CONTENTS

ABOUT A GIRL

Words and Music by
KURT COBAIN

Medium Rock

(1., D.S.) I need an eas-y friend, ___ I
(2.) I'm stand-ing in your line. ___ I

do, with an ear to ___ lend. I do think you
do hope you have the ___ time. ___ I do pick a

ACROSS THE UNIVERSE

Words and Music by JOHN LENNON
and PAUL McCARTNEY

Slowly and smoothly

Words are flow-ing out _ like end-less rain _ in-to a pa-per cup, _ they

slith-er while _ they pass, they slip a-way _ a-cross the u-ni-verse. _

Pools of sor-row, waves of joy are drift-ing through my o-pened mind, _ pos-

ANGIE

Words and Music by MICK JAGGER
and KEITH RICHARDS

AMERICAN PIE

Words and Music by
DON McLEAN

This - 'll be the day ___ that I ___ die. ___

1. Did you ___ write the book of love ___ and do you ___
2.-4. *(See additional lyrics)*

___ have faith in God a - bove? ___ If the Bi - ble tells ___

___ you so. ___ Now do you ___ be - lieve ___ in

D.S. al Coda

day   the mu - sic   died.   And they were sing - in'

CODA

this - 'll   be   the   day___   that   I____   die.____

Additional Lyrics

2. Now for ten years we've been on our own,
   And moss grows fat on a rollin' stone
   But that's not how it used to be
   When the jester sang for the king and queen
   In a coat he borrowed from James Dean
   And a voice that came from you and me
   Oh and while the king was looking down,
   The jester stole his thorny crown
   The courtroom was adjourned,
   No verdict was returned
   And while Lenin read a book on Marx
   The quartet practiced in the park
   And we sang dirges in the dark
   The day the music died
   We were singin'...bye-bye... etc.

3. Helter-skelter in the summer swelter
   The birds flew off with a fallout shelter
   Eight miles high and fallin' fast,
   It landed foul on the grass
   The players tried for a forward pass,
   With the jester on the sidelines in a cast
   Now the half-time air was sweet perfume
   While the sergeants played a marching tune
   We all got up to dance
   But we never got the chance
   'Cause the players tried to take the field,
   The marching band refused to yield
   Do you recall what was revealed
   The day the music died
   We started singin'... bye-bye...etc.

4. And there we were all in one place,
   A generation lost in space
   With no time left to start again
   So come on, Jack be nimble, Jack be quick,
   Jack Flash sat on a candlestick
   'Cause fire is the devil's only friend
   And as I watched him on the stage
   My hands were clenched in fits of rage
   No angel born in hell
   Could break that Satan's spell
   And as the flames climbed high into the night
   To light the sacrificial rite
   I saw Satan laughing with delight
   The day the music died
   He was singin'...bye-bye...etc.

AND I LOVE HER

Words and Music by JOHN LENNON
and PAUL McCARTNEY

Lyrics:

I give her all my love,
that's all I do.

She gives me ev-'ry-thing
and ten-der-ly.

Bright are the stars that shine,
dark is the sky.

D.S. al Coda

G#m   B

have you near me.

CODA

Gm

Instrumental solo
Bright are the stars

Dm   Gm   Dm

that shine, dark is the sky.

Gm   Dm   Bb

I know this love of mine will nev-er die.

ANNIE'S SONG

Words and Music by
JOHN DENVER

AT SEVENTEEN

Words and Music by
JANIS IAN

Moderately

Guitar (capo V) → G(add9) G Gmaj7 G6 G G(add9) G Gmaj7 G6 G

Keyboard → C(add9) C Cmaj7 C6 C C(add9) C Cmaj7 C6 C

mp

I

G(add9) G Gmaj7 G6 G Am11 Am7 E/A

C(add9) C Cmaj7 C6 C Dm11 Dm7 A/D

learned the truth at sev - en - teen, ___ that love was meant for beau -
brown - eyed girl in hand - me - downs ___ whose name I nev - er could ___
those of us who know ___ the pain ___ of val - en - tines that nev -

Am7 D7

Dm7 G7

- ty queens ___ and high school girls ___ with clear - skinned smiles ___ who
___ pro - nounce ___ said, "Pit - y, please, ___ the ones ___ who serve. ___ They
- er came, ___ and those whose names ___ were nev - er called ___ when

© 1975 (Renewed 2003) MINE MUSIC LTD.
All Rights for the U.S.A. and Canada Controlled and Administered by EMI APRIL MUSIC INC.
All Rights Reserved International Copyright Secured Used by Permission

BABE, I'M GONNA LEAVE YOU

Words and Music by ANNE BREDON,
JIMMY PAGE and ROBERT PLANT

Additional Lyrics

I know, I know, I know, I never, I never, I never, I never, I never leave you, baby
But I got to go away from this place, I've got to quit you.
Ooh, baby, baby, baby, baby
Baby, baby, baby, ooh don't you hear it callin'?
Woman, woman, I know, I know it's good to have you back again
And I know that one day, baby, it's really gonna grow, yes it is.
We gonna go walkin' through the park every day.
Hear what I say, every day.
Baby, it's really growin', you made me happy when skies were grey.
But now I've got to go away
Baby, baby, baby, baby
That's when it's callin' me
That's when it's callin' me back home...

BABY, I LOVE YOUR WAY

Words and Music by
PETER FRAMPTON

But don't hes-i-tate, _____ 'cause your

love _____ won't _____ wait. _____

D.S. al Coda

54

BAND ON THE RUN

Words and Music by
PAUL and LINDA McCARTNEY

BACK ON THE CHAIN GANG

Words and Music by
CHRISSIE HYNDE

We're back on the train. ___
Put us back on the train. ___

Oh, ___

back on the chain ___

1

___ gang.

2

Oh, ___

back on the chain gang.

The pow- ers that be that

force us to live like we do bring me to my knees

- pi - est days — of my life. _____

Like a break in the bat - tle _____ was your part, _____

oh, _____ in the wretch-ed life — of a lone - ly heart. _

_____ Now we're back on the train. _

Oh, _____ back on the chain ____ gang.

Repeat and Fade

BARELY BREATHING

Words and Music by
DUNCAN SHEIK

BE-BOP-A-LULA

Words and Music by TEX DAVIS
and GENE VINCENT

BEHIND BLUE EYES

Words and Music by
PETE TOWNSHEND

BLUE EYES CRYING IN THE RAIN

Words and Music by
FRED ROSE

BLACKBIRD

Words and Music by JOHN LENNON
and PAUL McCARTNEY

Black - bird sing - ing in the dead of night, _
Black - bird sing - ing in the dead of night, _

take these bro - ken wings _ and learn to fly; __
take these sunk - en eyes _ and learn to see; __

all your life _____ you were on - ly wait - ing for this mo - ment to a -
all your life _____ you were on - ly wait - ing for this mo - ment to be

BLOWIN' IN THE WIND

Words and Music by
BOB DYLAN

CANDLE IN THE WIND

Words and Music by ELTON JOHN
and BERNIE TAUPIN

Good-bye Nor - ma Jean, _____ though I nev - er knew you _____ at all
Lone - li - ness _____ was tough, _____ the tough-est role you ev - er played.

you had the grace to hold your-self _____ while those a - round _____ you crawled. _____
Hol - ly-wood cre - at - ed a su - per - star _____ and pain was the price you paid. _____

They crawled out of the wood-work
E - ven when you died,

Good-bye Nor - ma Jean, _____ though I nev - er _____ knew you _____ at all, you had the grace to hold your - self _____ while those a - round _____ you crawled. _____

96

CRAZY LITTLE THING CALLED LOVE

Words and Music by
FREDDIE MERCURY

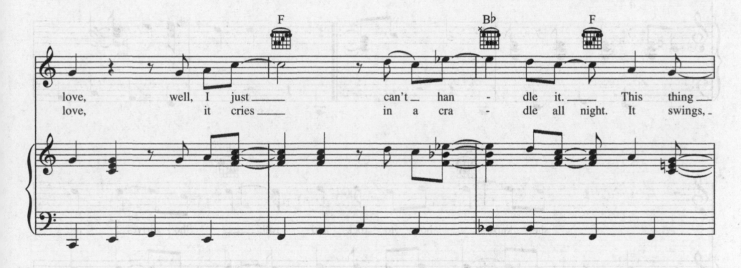

mo - tor bike __ un - til I'm read - y.   Cra - zy lit - tle thing called

love.

I got - ta be cool, ____ re - lax, ___

___ a - get hip, ___ a - get on my tracks. Take a

back seat, ____ hitch - hike ____ to take a lit - tle long _ ride _ on my

CHICAGO

Words and Music by
GRAHAM NASH

* *Male vocal written at actual pitch.*

(Sittin' On)
THE DOCK OF THE BAY

Words and Music by STEVE CROPPER
and OTIS REDDING

CRYING

Words and Music by ROY ORBISON
and JOE MELSON

DO YOU BELIEVE IN MAGIC

Words and Music by
JOHN SEBASTIAN

FAST CAR

Words and Music by
TRACY CHAPMAN

Moderately

Play 4 times

You got a fast___ car. I want a tick-et to an-y-where.

You got a fast___ car. I got a plan to get us out of here. I've been

May-be we make a deal.___ May-be to-geth-er we can get some - where.___

work-ing at the con-ven-ience store. Man-aged to save just a lit-tle bit of mon-ey.

An-y place is bet-ter.___ Start-ing from ze-ro, got noth-ing to lose.

Won't have to drive too far, just cross the bor-der and in-to the cit-y.

124

FREE BIRD

Words and Music by ALLEN COLLINS
and RONNIE VAN ZANT

FREE FALLIN'

Words and Music by TOM PETTY
and JEFF LYNNE

134

FRIENDS IN LOW PLACES

Words and Music by DeWAYNE BLACKWELL
and EARL BUD LEE

Well, I

I've got friends __ in low plac - es where the

whis - key __ drowns __ and the beer __ chas - es my blues __

Low effort - this is sheet music, image-dominant page.

GIRL

Words and Music by JOHN LENNON
and PAUL McCARTNEY

HAVE YOU EVER REALLY LOVED A WOMAN?

from the Motion Picture DON JUAN DeMARCO

Words and Music by BRYAN ADAMS,
MICHAEL KAMEN and ROBERT JOHN "MUTT" LANGE

HELP ME MAKE IT
THROUGH THE NIGHT

HELP ME MAKE IT THROUGH THE NIGHT

Words and Music by
KRIS KRISTOFFERSON

Take the rib-bon from your
Come and lay down by my
Yes-ter-day is dead and

hair,
side
gone

Shake it
Till the
And to -

HELPLESSLY HOPING

Words and Music by
STEPHEN STILLS

They are one _____ per - son, they are two _____ a - lone, _____ they are three _____ to - geth - er, they are for _____ each oth - er.

HOMEWARD BOUND

Words and Music by
PAUL SIMON

I AM A MAN OF CONSTANT SORROW

featured in O BROTHER, WHERE ART THOU?

Words and Music by
CARTER STANLEY

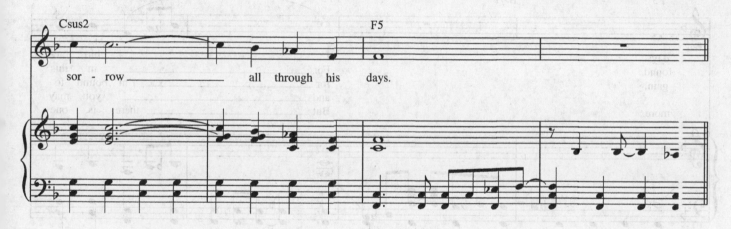

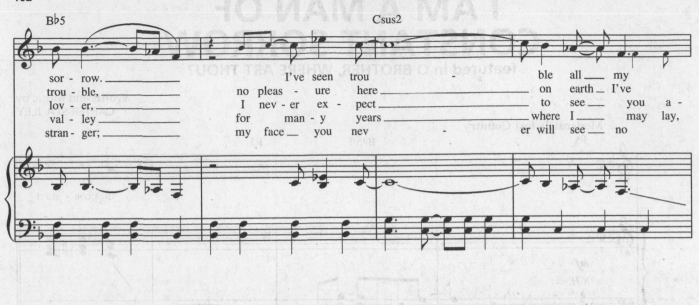

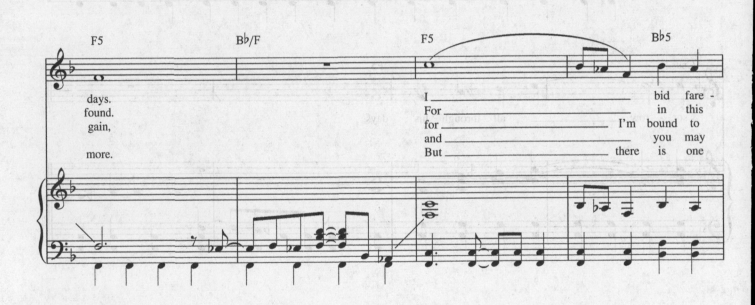

I'LL HAVE TO SAY I LOVE YOU
IN A SONG

Words and Music by
JIM CROCE

LANDSLIDE

Words and Music by
STEVIE NICKS

LAYLA

Words and Music by ERIC CLAPTON
and JIM GORDON

What will you do___ when you get lone-ly
I tried___ to give___ you con-so-la-tion
So make___ the best___ of the sit-u-a-tion

*Recorded a whole step lower.

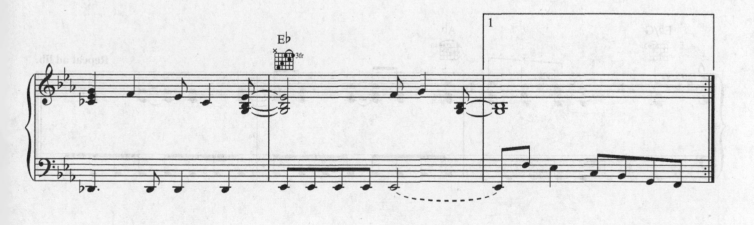

LEAVING ON A JET PLANE

Words and Music by
JOHN DENVER

LEADER OF THE BAND

Words and Music by
DAN FOGELBERG

186

D.S. al Coda

CODA

nough.   The lead - er of the band __ is tired __ and __ his

LOVER, YOU SHOULD'VE COME OVER

Words and Music by
JEFF BUCKLEY

bro - ken down and hun - gry for your love _____ with no way to

feed it. _____ Where are ___ you ___ to -

night? You know how much I need it. _____

Too young to hold on, too old ___ to break free and

MICHELLE

Words and Music by JOHN LENNON
and PAUL McCARTNEY

MORE THAN A FEELING

Words and Music by
TOM SCHOLZ

When I'm tired __ and think-ing cold, I hide in my mu - sic, for-

NIGHT MOVES

Words and Music by
BOB SEGER

And we'd steal a - way ev -'ry chance we could,

to the back room, to the al - ley, or the trust - y woods. _____

I used her, she used me, __ but nei - ther one cared. _____

We were get - tin' our share, __ work - in' on our night moves, _____

MORE THAN WORDS

Words and Music by NUNO BETTENCOURT
and GARY CHERONE

Say - in' "I ___ love ___ you" is
Now that I've ___ tried ___ to

not the words ___ I want ___ to ___ hear ___ from you. ___ It's not that I ___
talk to you ___ and make ___ you un - der - stand, ___ all ___ you ___

Recorded a half step lower.

222

NIGHTS IN WHITE SATIN

Words and Music by
JUSTIN HAYWARD

SOMEBODY TO LOVE

Words and Music by
DARBY SLICK

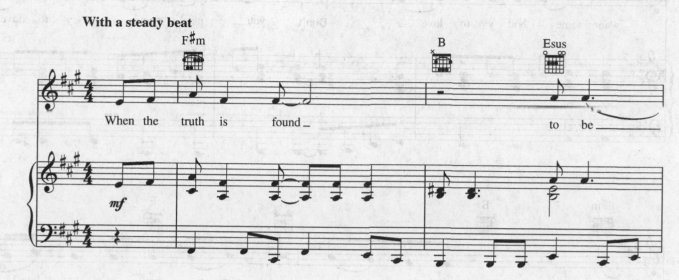

NORWEGIAN WOOD
(This Bird Has Flown)

Words and Music by JOHN LENNON
and PAUL McCARTNEY

ONLY WANNA BE WITH YOU

Words and Music by DARIUS CARLOS RUCKER,
EVERETT DEAN FELBER, MARK WILLIAM BRYAN
and JAMES GEORGE SONEFELD

OUR HOUSE

Words and Music by
GRAHAM NASH

I'll light the fire; ___ you place the flow-ers in the vase ___ that you bought ___ to-day. ___

Star-ing at ___ the fire

SCARBOROUGH FAIR

Arrangement and original counter melody by
PAUL SIMON and ARTHUR GARFUNKEL

Moderately slow

SEVEN BRIDGES ROAD

Words and Music by
STEPHEN T. YOUNG

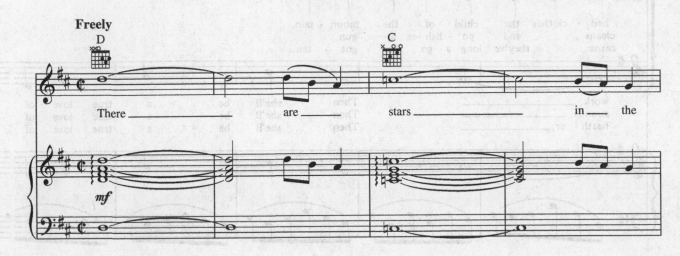

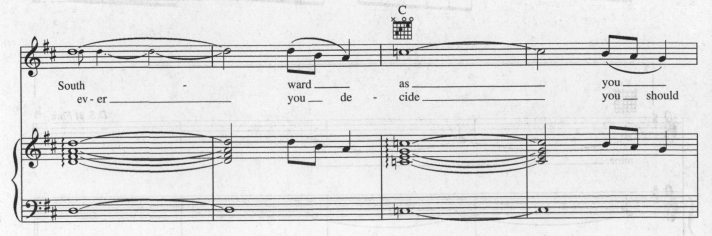

Bright Country

SOUTHERN CROSS

Words and Music by STEPHEN STILLS,
RICHARD CURTIS and MICHAEL CURTIS

THE SPACE BETWEEN

Words and Music by DAVID J. MATTHEWS
and GLEN BALLARD

Additional Lyrics

2. The rain that falls splashed in your heart,
Ran like sadness down the window into your room.

3. The space between our wicked lies is where
We hope to keep safe from pain.

4. Take my hand 'cause
We're walking out of here.

5. Oh, right out of here.
Love is all we need, dear.

SWEET HOME CHICAGO

Words and Music by
ROBERT JOHNSON

* *Recorded a half step lower.*

TAKE ME HOME, COUNTRY ROADS

Words and Music by JOHN DENVER,
BILL DANOFF and TAFFY NIVERT

SWEET TALKIN' WOMAN

Words and Music by
JEFF LYNNE

TEACH YOUR CHILDREN

Words and Music by
GRAHAM NASH

TEARS IN HEAVEN

Words and Music by ERIC CLAPTON
and WILL JENNINGS

TIME IN A BOTTLE

Words and Music by
JIM CROCE

find them. _____ I've

looked a-round e-nough to know that you're the one I want to go through

time with. If

I had a box just for wish-es _____ and

TO BE WITH YOU

Words and Music by ERIC MARTIN
and DAVID GRAHAME

UP ON THE ROOF

Words and Music by GERRY GOFFIN
and CAROLE KING

WAKE UP LITTLE SUSIE

Words and Music by BOUDLEAUX BRYANT
and FELICE BRYANT

WANTED DEAD OR ALIVE

Words and Music by JON BON JOVI
and RICHIE SAMBORA

Csus G   F   D   Csus G   **To Coda** ⊕

cow-boy,   on a steel horse. I ride.   I'm want-ed, (want - ed,) ___

D   Csus G   D

dead or a - live. ___   Want-ed, (want - ed,) ___   dead or a - live. ___

N.C.

1

Some -

WONDERFUL TONIGHT

Words and Music by
ERIC CLAPTON

It's late in the eve — ning; she's won-d'ring what clothes
We go to a par — ty, and ev-'ry-one turns
It's time to go home now, and I've got an ach-

— to wear. She puts on her make — up
to see this beau-ti-ful la — dy
-ing head. So I give her the car keys,

and brush-es her long blonde hair. And then she asks
is walk-ing a-round with me. And then she asks
and she helps me to bed. And then I tell

WONDERWALL

Words and Music by
NOEL GALLAGHER

YOU'VE GOT A FRIEND

Words and Music by
CAROLE KING

*Vocal harmony sung 2nd time only

YOU'RE IN MY HEART

Words and Music by
ROD STEWART

I did-n't know ___ what day it was ___ when you walked ___

I took all ___ those hab-its of yours that in the be -

You're ev-'ry love song ever writ-ten, but, hon-ey, what

leave. But I bite my lip and turn a-round, 'cause you're the warm-

do you see in me? You're in my heart;

-est thing I've ev-er found. You're in my heart;

you're in my soul. You'd be my breath should I grow old. You are my lov-

-er; you're my best friend. You're in my soul.